# El bosque

por Emma Casey

Every effort has been made to secure permission and provide appropriate credit for photographic material. The publisher deeply regrets any omission and pledges to correct errors called to its attention in subsequent editions.

Unless otherwise acknowledged, all photographs are the property of Pearson.

Photo locations denoted as follows: Top (T), Center (C), Bottom (B), Left (L), Right (R), Background (Bkgd)

CVR ©Gregory K. Scott/Photo Researchers, Inc.; 1 ©Nikki Heikki/OSF/Animals Animals/ Earth Scenes; 3 ©Laura Ciapponi/Getty Images; 4 ©Nikki Heikki/OSF/Animals Animals/ Earth Scenes; 5 ©Mark Jones/Animals Animals/Earth Scenes; 6 ©Stephen Dalton/Photo Researchers, Inc.; 7 ©Gregory K. Scott/Photo Researchers, Inc.; 8 ©Johnny Johnson/ Animals Animals/Earth Scenes

ISBN 13: 978-0-328-41095-8
ISBN 10:     0-328-41095-0

**Copyright © Pearson Education, Inc. or its affiliate(s). All Rights Reserved.**
Printed in the United States of America. This publication is protected by copyright and permission should be obtained from the publisher prior to any prohibited reproduction, storage in a retrieval system, or transmission in any form or by any means, electronic, mechanical, photocopying, recording, or likewise. For information regarding permission(s), write to: Pearson School Rights and Permissions, One Lake Street, Upper Saddle River, New Jersey 07458.

Pearson and Scott Foresman are trademarks, in the U.S. and/or other countries, of Pearson Education, Inc. or its affiliate(s).

2 3 4 5 6 7 8 9 10 V010 17 16 15 14 13 12 11 10

Los árboles viven en el bosque.

Las plantas viven en el bosque.

Los pájaros viven en el bosque.

Los insectos viven en el bosque.

Los venados viven en el bosque.

Los osos viven en el bosque.